YOU & YOUR CHILD
PRIMARY EDUCATION

First published 1999

Letts Educational
Aldine House
Aldine Place
London W12 8AW
Telephone 020 8740 2266

Text: © BPP (Letts Educational) Ltd 1999

Author: Tony Eaude
Series editor: Roy Blatchford
Project manager: Alex Edmonds
Editorial assistance: Tanya Solomons

Design and illustrations: © BPP (Letts Educational) Ltd 1999
Design by Peter Laws
Illustrations by Madeleine Hardy
Cover design by Peter Laws

British Library Cataloguing in Publication Data
A CIP record for this book is available at the British Library.

ISBN 185758 9777

Colour Reproduction by PDQ Repro Limited, Bungay, Suffolk.
Printed and bound in Italy

Letts Educational is the trading name of BPP (Letts Educational) Ltd

Letts Educational would like to thank all the parents who sent in their tips for educating children
and who wrote with such enthusiasm about parenthood.

YOU & YOUR CHILD
PRIMARY EDUCATION

Tony Eaude

Contents

Words in **bold** are defined in the glossary at the back of this book.

"Do not confine your children to your own learning for they were born in different time."

HEBREW PROVERB

Dear Parent,

What happens at nursery and in primary school is vital to your child's education. What you do at home is just as important.

It's never too soon to start supporting your child's learning. The time that you spend with your child in the primary years gives him or her a foundation that lasts a lifetime. Make the most of every opportunity for you and your child to enjoy learning together.

You don't need to be an expert. You do need to be enthusiastic. The time you invest at home – talking about homework projects, practising skills, playing games – will help your child achieve all through primary and secondary school and open up opportunities for him or her in the future.

This book is one in a major new series from Letts. It will help you support your child, with information about what to look for in a good primary school. It tells you how schools help children learn throughout the primary curriculum, and advises on how you can help your child get the best out of primary school, including homework challenges, extra-curricular activities and school trips.

I hope you enjoy sharing primary learning with your child. The important thing is to make learning fun!

Roy Blatchford.

ROY BLATCHFORD
Series editor

What makes a good primary school?

Primary schools are often very special places. Children and parents remember them with great affection as centres of the village, community or local area.

There are over 25,000 primary schools in England and Wales and they range in size from tiny village schools with only one class to big schools with over 600 pupils in some towns and cities. Most have between 100 and 250 pupils, with between four and ten classes.

Primary schools are also surprisingly different in style. The type of school usually reflects the local community. But, as parents exercise their choice about where to send their child, some schools draw their pupils from a wider area, especially in big cities.

What different types of school are there?

THERE ARE TWO MAIN TYPES OF SCHOOL:

1 Church schools are schools with a religious foundation – mostly Church of England, but also Roman Catholic and other religious groups such as Jews and, more recently, Muslims. The main differences between Church schools and other schools are in admissions (who goes to the school) and the way that religious education (R.E.) is taught.

2 Community schools which are funded and controlled by **Local Education Authorities (LEAs)**. There are also a few other types of school, such as Foundation schools (previously known as Grant-maintained schools), which are directly funded by the government and are independent of LEAs.

All these schools follow the **National Curriculum**.

At what age do children start and leave primary school?

The age group covered by primary schools is from four or five to 11 years old. Some schools cover the whole age range, others only part of it. Some have a nursery attached for three- to five-year-olds, others not.

Children usually move to secondary school at age 11. In some areas there are first schools, for the early years of primary, and middle schools which overlap with the secondary age range.

The age of admission varies. Usually children start at the beginning of the term in which their fifth birthday occurs. Recently, there has been pressure to get children into school younger. Generally, your child may do best to stay in good pre-school provision if he or she is settled there.

Parent tip

"Remember that all schools have different strengths. It's a good idea to start finding out about local schools early."

What is special about primary education?

Primary schools are proud of a tradition that recognises that young children:

- ✔ have needs that are different from those of older children

- ✔ benefit from teaching based with mainly one teacher and class

- ✔ flourish where their learning needs are considered as a whole, instead of in little blocks

- ✔ learn best and grow personally by relating well with other people

> **Parent tip**
>
> "Be prepared to approach the teacher and don't be afraid to ask if you're not sure about something or you want more information."

In primary schools the curriculum is not as divided into separate subjects as at secondary school. Teachers can go into topics (see page 35) in more depth. Recently primary schools have moved towards working more in subjects, with more **setting** and **streaming**, especially in the **core subjects** of English, maths and science.

Learning to read, write and do maths is vital in the Early Years (when your child is in nursery or the Reception class). As well as these skills, primary schools usually place a strong emphasis on music, art and other creative subjects. However, the range of options and specialisms is narrower than in secondary schools.

A primary teacher has a close relationship with each child and will know a lot about his or her strengths or problems. Most children need and enjoy the challenge and opportunities offered by new experiences and relationships. Some will also need a haven away from difficulties outside, even if only for a short time. The school's task is to provide what your child needs at any time.

When your child starts school he or she will usually find primary school bigger and less personal than nursery or pre-school. Teachers have big classes – often up to 30 with five- to seven-year-olds, and more for older children. If you want to know something, or make a suggestion, don't be afraid to ask. The teacher will usually be approachable, but you may need to make the first step.

Which school should my child go to?

You will probably want your child to go to a primary school close to home. Remember that having friends who live nearby, travelling to school and being part of a local community are all aspects of your child's experience.

If you live in a rural area, you may have little choice of schools, especially if you have no transport. In towns and cities there may be more options.

> **Parent quote**
>
> "We had to move out of the city and I think it was leaving her school and the friends she made there that was hardest for her."

The reasons you may want your child to go to a school other than your local one may be:

- ✔ religious – if you want your child to go to a school with a religious basis

- ✔ personal – such as if someone in your family went to a particular school, you work nearby or it fits well with your own friendship or work patterns

- ✔ you have heard that a particular school is a good one

The next two chapters will help you find out more about local schools.

How can I find out what a school is like?

Schools offer different strengths and approaches. You need to decide which school suits you and your child best. Don't go just on a school's reputation. What your friends and neighbours – or the press – think may be different from your own judgement. It is important that you feel comfortable with the ethos and atmosphere of the school.

Which school will suit my child?

✔ See if there is a link with your child's nursery or pre-school which would provide good continuity and the chance for friendships to continue into primary school.

✔ Look at the school **prospectus** or **brochure** and the report by **OFSTED (Office for Standards in Education)** inspectors.

✔ Above all, go and visit and judge for yourself.

> **Parent tip**
>
> "We found that visiting prospective schools really helped. Some schools that looked good on paper just didn't feel right."

Where do I get the prospectus and OFSTED report?

Every school will provide a prospectus and a summary of the main findings of the OFSTED report free of charge. You probably won't need the full OFSTED report. They are quite long and you must pay the cost of photocopying. Call in, write to or phone up the school. Schools will probably be able to give you other documents which might help you come to a decision on schools if you ask, such as a policy on special educational needs or bullying.

OFSTED reports are available in the local library or on the Internet. (There is a list of useful addresses and websites at the end of this book.)

What will the prospectus tell me?

The school produces this to explain:

✔ its aims and objectives

✔ how the school is organised

✔ its approach to teaching

✔ its pastoral care system (how it looks after children and keeps them safe)

✔ extras that the school offers

✔ everyday things like dates, times, rules and lunch arrangements

Parent quote

"I wasn't too worried about whether it was a church school or not, but I heard from my neighbours that it was friendly and that the results were very good."

What is an OFSTED report?

All schools have been inspected in the last four years by an OFSTED team appointed by the government. In future, this will happen every six years. OFSTED inspectors are independent people, mostly teachers or advisers, who examine and judge all aspects of the school. Church schools have a separate report on worship and/or religious education.

What is a report like?

The report includes a summary of the school's strengths and weaknesses and key points for action.

THE MAIN COMMENTS CONCERN:

- ✔ quality of education

- ✔ educational standards achieved

- ✔ how efficiently resources are used

- ✔ children's spiritual, moral, social and cultural development

How much notice should I take of OFSTED?

Don't make a decision on a school purely on the report. Sometimes schools do better or worse under the pressure of inspection than expected. New staff or approaches may have changed things. The report should not be a substitute for visiting and getting the feel of the school.

The report includes statistics comparing achievement levels, attendance and other areas with other local and national schools. Treat these with some caution. They may not necessarily tell you whether a school is a good school or not.

The language of these reports is quite heavy-going but OFSTED is trying to make the reports more user-friendly. If the school was judged to need 'special measures' or had 'serious weaknesses', this does not necessarily mean your child will not do well there, but you should look closely to see what the school has done to remedy these.

What should I look for?

You will be surprised how much you find out by spending a short while in a school. Don't just wander in, of course. Make an appointment to look round, and take your child with you if you want.

THINGS TO NOTICE AROUND THE SCHOOL:

✔ Are the classrooms interesting and colourful with children's work valued and well presented?

✔ Are there good facilities for play? And for learning?

✔ Is the reception area welcoming and well organised?

✔ Are the buildings and grounds well looked after? Is there a lot of graffiti or litter?

It is especially important to consider the relationships between people...

✔ Are children happy, welcoming and settled?

✔ Is the standard of behaviour and care appropriate?

✔ Do adults and children talk politely and pleasantly to each other?

If you can, meet the headteacher who should be happy to explain how the school works, and what it aims to achieve. Of course, he or she can't say everything and won't always point out problems, so be prepared to ask questions. Ask to visit a class briefly.

Good classrooms look interesting and have a purposeful and quiet (but not silent) atmosphere.

What should I ask?

Look at the prospectus first and work out in advance what you want to ask. This may include questions about:

✔ how classes are organised and what size they are

✔ how children are taught

✔ any particular strengths of the school

✔ discipline and how bullying is dealt with

✔ how much parents are expected to be involved

You may also like to discuss specific things such as how R.E. or sport are taught, lunch arrangements or the homework policy. But over all, try to get the feel of whether your child will thrive and learn at this school.

Work out if there is anything else you feel that you need to know about the school.

Parent tip

"I've always found that the best thing to go by is the way you feel about a school – trust your intuition."

What OFSTED reports might say:

🖊 'Expectations are high for behaviour but frequently low for academic achievement.'

🖊 'The school provides a supportive environment in which pupils have the opportunity to enjoy school life, develop their confidence and concentrate on their learning.'

🖊 'Current strengths are identified in literacy, history and music with some weaknesses in geography and design technology.'

🖊 'In Year 6, the pupils show interest and work quietly and carefully. Elsewhere pupils' attitudes are more variable.'

How do I get my child into the school I want?

Getting your child into the primary school you want can be easy, or very complicated. Often, parents just fill in one form, but sometimes it can be a real battle. Remember:

✔ find out early what to do

✔ don't just assume you'll be able to get your child into a particular school

✔ don't be afraid to ask

At what age will my child start?

This is complicated! Each LEA has a policy. These can differ enormously and sometimes church schools can differ from other schools in the same LEA.

The most common starting age is when children are **'rising fives'**. This means the term in which your child is five. In some areas this term can be part-time, but it is usually full-time. In a few LEAs your child will not start until the term after he or she is five.

In many LEAs children start in the September before they are five. This means that some children are only just four. Just to make it even more confusing, many schools take children earlier than they have to, to keep their numbers up.

Do not assume that starting your child in primary school very young is the best option. In this country parents tend to be encouraged to get their children into school very young. Starting school can be daunting for a young child and a Reception class curriculum may not be right for him or her. It may suit your child far better to stay at pre-school with a more relaxed curriculum and higher staffing levels.

Can my child go to whichever school I choose?

Not necessarily. If a school is full, your child may not get a place. The LEA will then offer your child a place in another local school.

Every house is in the **catchment area** of at least one school. This does not mean you have to send your child there, just that you will get priority if you do.

> ### Parent tip
>
> "Don't be afraid to ask teachers, or any educational professional, about things that are worrying you. I didn't and I really wish I had done now."

In rural areas schools are often less full, so it is more likely you will get your preference. In towns and cities, it can be much harder. This is partly because it is easier for parents to 'vote with their feet', and partly because schools are much keener to keep their numbers up than they used to be.

Who decides on places if a school is full?

All LEAs have admission policies to decide who goes where when schools are over-subscribed. It is even more complicated with church aided schools which have their own admission policies, often based on whichever church they are linked to. It is preferable to find out the situation when your child is still only two or three years old, since it may influence your choice of pre-school. Remember that pre-schools often have separate admission policies from primary schools, even when they are linked.

If you are moving into another area, contact the new LEA as soon as you can. You can get the admission policy and a list of local schools. Apply for a place as soon as your move is confirmed.

A word of warning! Moving children from school to school is not sensible. If you move, your child should be able to settle down soon. But too much moving does cause disruption. Avoid doing so without good reason.

When will I know if my child has a place?

This varies between LEAs and between schools. In some areas there may be uncertainty until just before a child is due to start. Remember to keep asking for an answer from the education department or the school. Don't be put off!

If you do not get your first choice, your child will be offered a place at another school. If you feel strongly, then appeal. It is not too daunting a process but it does mean more uncertainty. It is worth thinking whether it is really that important to get into your first choice school.

Once my child has a place, what next?

Most schools arrange times for parents and children to visit before the school term starts. Do so with your child if you can. It will reduce the anxieties you both have.

You can avoid a lot of worry or unhappiness during the first few weeks of school simply by careful attention to detail. Finding out about rules and expectations at the school means that our child will feel fully prepared for the big 'first day' at school.

Parent tips and quotes

"Don't rush your child into school very young, it can put too much pressure on him or her."

"We had a terrible time and had to go to appeal. In the end we got her in, but I wish we'd known earlier about all the rules and regulations."

Examples of questions to ask once your child has got a place

Q What do the children need? Is there a uniform or dress code?

A Look in the prospectus or check with the teacher.

Q What should I do if my child struggles with shoe-laces or buttons?

A Velcro-fastening shoes and tracksuit bottoms can make life much easier.

Q What are the arrangements for eating dinners or snacks? Is there a water fountain?

A Ask in the school office or at the introductory visit.

Q Where do children hang their coats? Where are the toilets?

A Find out and go, with your child, to have a look.

How can I prepare my child for primary school?

As a parent, you already do a lot to help your child's education. Don't get too worried about doing a lot more to get your child 'ready for school'.

What work should my child have covered?

Whatever is written here won't stop you being anxious about how good your child is at his or her work. Soon after your child starts the teacher will do a **Baseline Assessment**. You and your friends will be keen to make sure your children do well. But don't over-prepare your child for this.

Sometimes education seems like a race, but too much pressure can be counter-productive, especially in the Early Years. Don't worry too much about what your child can or can't do. If you are too anxious, your child will pick this up and become anxious as well. Children start school at different stages and with varying abilities, and they progress at different speeds. Some children start school reading fluently and writing well – others don't.

Starting school

- ✔ talk with and listen to your child, especially about any worries he or she has

- ✔ read to and with your child

- ✔ spend time enjoying your child's company

- ✔ try to help your child be interested and observant

- ✔ encourage independence and thoughtfulness

Parent tip

"Above all, enjoy your child's primary years. It's amazing how quickly they pass and how much fun they are."

What information should I pass on to the school?

Parent quote

"He had a difficult first few weeks at dinner time because he hadn't really learnt how to cut up his food, so he took ages to finish his lunch."

If your child has needs requiring adaptations or special help, tell the school well in advance of starting. If there are specific problems to do with access of one parent, or any legal argument, make sure the school knows – in confidence if necessary. The school does need to know in order to do the best for your child.

What happens at home affects schoolwork, and the other way round.

The school will give you forms to fill in giving details of both you and your child. Use them to tell the school what they need to know, especially if your child has physical or educational needs requiring:

✔ medication or care with allergies

✔ adaptations or extra help

You may have other records or requests, such as health records or special food requirements to pass on from pre-school.

What about the first few weeks at school?

Remember to listen and respond to your child's questions or worries. It is normal for children to be anxious. Don't be put off if, when you ask your child what happened at school, the answer is 'Nothing' or 'Just played'. Probably he or she just doesn't want to talk about work, or thinks you won't really understand. But keep showing an interest!

It is a big moment when a child starts primary school – for your child and for you! You have to find a suitable balance between being interested and supportive and letting go.

Introducing yourself to the teacher gives you the chance to check that he or she knows any specific medical needs and important issues like who drops off or picks up your child.

Parent tip

"Even before he or she starts school, get into routines with your child to give some structure to the day."

From the beginning:

• Start off with good routines – like getting your child to school on time and being prompt to pick him or her up.

• Watch out for tiredness, especially early on. Don't expect your child to do too much after school. It is hard work! He or she may be less well-behaved or co-operative than usual.

• Listen to what your child says about friendships and the playground. This is often the hardest part of the day for young children, especially boys. You may need to talk about how to cope with a new situation. A good start is important not just because you want your child to be happy, but because it lays a good foundation for future learning.

• Be practical and tolerant. Learning can be a messy business – involving clay and paint and water – so don't send your child to school dressed up for a party!

Is there a problem when children change classes?

Many parents get very concerned about a change of teacher. When children are very young, continuity of teacher and of friendships is especially important. Constant chopping and changing doesn't help. But one aspect of growing up is for your child to manage new approaches and new friendships. Schools work hard to ensure that children build on the skills and interests they have developed previously.

As your child goes through primary school, your support is vital, especially in difficult areas such as:

- ✔ friendships

- ✔ homework

- ✔ behaviour and discipline

Above all, don't get too anxious or protective.

Encourage and praise your child's successes and share the excitement of learning.

Parent quote

"When my daughter started school, she found it very easy because all her friends except one had gone on with her from the nursery."

Remember!

- ✔ listen and attend to your child's questions or worries
- ✔ tell the school about your child, especially when help may be needed
- ✔ don't worry if your child seems to be a bit 'behind'
- ✔ set up good routines
- ✔ watch out for tiredness
- ✔ introduce yourself to the teacher
- ✔ enjoy your child's primary years

What will my child learn at primary school?

What is the curriculum?

The curriculum sets out what is taught at school. Schools have different approaches and teaching methods. About ten years ago, the government introduced the National Curriculum to improve consistency and to raise standards. More recently, the government brought in the **Literacy Hour** and the **Daily Maths Lesson**. These changes squeeze the time available for science, physical education (P.E.), art and music. There is a lot of discussion about how best to teach primary school children. The main issue is how much to concentrate on the core subjects and how much to provide a wide range of other subjects. More changes are certain with the curriculum under constant review.

> ### Parent tip
>
> "Try to encourage your child in the creative subjects, not just the basics."

> ### Parent quote
>
> "Jason enjoyed drawing and we encouraged him in that as much as in maths and science."

DO I NEED TO KNOW ABOUT THESE CHANGES?

Yes and no. No, since most schools try to teach children as well as possible anyway and provide a wide range of the curriculum. Yes, because you will help your child to do better if you can support his or her learning by reinforcing the work done at school and filling in areas not covered.

WHAT IS THE LITERACY HOUR?

Recently, almost all schools have started the Literacy Hour. A full hour each day is devoted mainly to reading with a clearly set-out approach, based on whole-class teaching and group work. This has been controversial. Some children and teachers like the very structured set-up and emphasis on phonics (sounding words out). Critics worry about the lack of time for speaking and listening and the fact that it limits the amount of time spent on other subjects.

WHAT IS THE DAILY MATHS LESSON?

In September 1999, schools introduced a Daily Maths Lesson to try to raise the level of achievement in mathematics. This is more flexible than the Literacy Hour and entails less change because it is closer to what schools have been doing for many years. Early signs are that it provides a less rigid structure for children and teachers and offers a welcome emphasis on the basics of maths.

I've heard about reading schemes. What are they?

Reading schemes are sets of graded reading books. They show how difficult a book is, but they can be a bit dull and encourage children to be competitive and to race on too quickly. Most schools use reading schemes to some extent, but try to have a range of more interesting picture and story books used alongside them.

Don't get anxious about reading schemes. Children need to read all sorts of texts to increase their skills and confidence. Encourage your child to read a wide range of books.

What about computers?

Computers can be a very effective way of teaching in some subjects, but children can have limited access to computers at school. The government is keen to improve the way primary schools teach using **Information and Communications Technology (I.C.T.)**. They are spending a lot of money on the National Grid for Learning (NGfL) to update computers and to help teachers and parents. You can find information about I.C.T. and links to other useful websites by logging onto the NGfL site on the Internet at www.ngfl.gov.uk. The sites are carefully checked to make sure they are safe for children, and of a high quality. Many children with special educational needs and able or gifted children particularly can benefit from using computers. Your child can gain a great deal if you have a computer at home.

Parent quote

"If you have a computer at home, make good use of it. My wife and I were a bit frightened of all the technology and I regret the fact that we didn't get to grips with it. Our daughter would have benefitted from using the computer."

Where does science fit in?

Your child will love learning about the world. The best work in science involves observation and experiment, including a lot of practical work. Many topics have a strong science base, with your child learning about space or soil, about electricity or minibeasts. Early play helps children learn scientific concepts. At the older end, your child will learn to make a hypothesis (the starting point of a scientific investigation) and test it out.

How important are art, music, P.E. and other subjects?

Young children learn by doing and making. They need a broad and varied curriculum. So these areas are important to build self-confidence and develop a wide range of creative abilities.

Parent quote

"She always just said she'd been painting and playing. It was only when I went to the first parents' evening that I got any sense of how many different things there were to do."

Do schools teach religious education?

All schools have to teach religious education, but it is not officially part of the National Curriculum. In most schools, there is a locally **Agreed Syllabus** and children are taught about different religions and religious ideas. In Church schools, the curriculum will probably be more explicitly Christian. Parents have the right to withdraw children from R.E. but this rarely happens.

Schools must have an act of collective worship each day. Normally this is an assembly for the whole or part of the school. Usually there is a story, a song and sometimes a prayer, often led by the headteacher or another teacher, or the local vicar. Sometimes this takes place in class.

What about sex education?

All schools must have a policy on sex education. This is usually fairly general with younger children and more explicit when children are nine or ten. Because this is a sensitive area, schools inform parents in advance and say what will be taught. Almost all parents are happy for the school to provide this.

Remember!

✔ encourage your child to read a wide range of books

✔ encourage your child in creative subjects as well as the basics

✔ if you have a computer at home, make good use of it

✔ find out about R.E. and sex education in your child's school, especially if you have questions

Parent quotes

"As a Sikh, I made it my business to find out about how the school taught R.E. and sex education. Then I could feel confident about allowing my son to attend the classes."

"He is very secretive – when pressed he assures me I probably wouldn't understand the complexity of his lessons."

How are primary schools organised?

Almost all primary schools are divided into classes where your child will spend most of his or her time. Usually, one teacher teaches your child for every subject each year up to the age of seven or eight. In the older primary years, this may change for some subjects but the class teacher still keeps a close link with a class.

Do children work in separate groups for some subjects?

Classes are split up because:

- ✔ teachers exchange groups because one teacher has a particular skill, for example in sport or music

- ✔ children are put into groups of roughly the same ability. This is called setting, for particular subjects, or streaming for all subjects. Setting is becoming more common especially in big schools with a wide spread of ability

- ✔ children have extra help, usually because they speak English as an additional language or if they have special educational needs. This is covered further in Chapter Eight.

What is a typical classroom like?

A typical primary classroom will have:

✔ an area for the whole class to sit and listen to stories and take the register

✔ a book corner

✔ tables organised so that children sit in groups

✔ an area with a computer

✔ areas with interesting items on topics the class is studying

✔ an area for dressing up and often for sand and water play, especially in Reception classes

Classrooms are usually attractive, colourful and interesting so children are encouraged to handle things and try them out.

Parent tip

"My daughter's classroom is always so colourful. You can tell a lot about a teacher from the way he or she organises the room."

What is a typical day like?

This varies but each normal day will include:

- welcoming everyone and taking the register

- assembly with other classes or the class thinking quietly together

- the Literacy Hour where children work as a whole class and in groups mainly on reading

- the Daily Maths Lesson, again partly as a whole class, partly in groups, working on maths

- a playtime in mid-morning

- a break of an hour or so for lunch

Your child will not study all the subjects every day, but during each week will do science, (usually with some practical work), P.E. (two or three times a week), music, R.E., art, history and geography.

You can see how much schools have to fit in!

What is a topic?

Most classes study a topic for a term or half a term. Young children learn best when they make links, and don't jump too much between different subjects. So different lessons, such as history and geography, are often combined within topics.

Topics might be about anything from 'Light' to 'The Vikings', from 'Harvest' to 'Famous People'. Schools plan topics over a period of time, often two years. Usually, the teacher sends out a list of the different areas to be covered in a term. This helps you know about and extend your child's schoolwork.

Do children get a chance to play?

Play is important for four- and five-year-olds especially — it helps them learn to investigate and discover for themselves. The pressure to cover the whole curriculum means that children play much less than they used to. So four-year-olds may often be better off in nursery than the Reception class.

Parent quote

"I found it really helpful when – in the end – the school sent home a list of what they were covering that term in the topic."

What about my child at the older end of primary school?

As a child progresses through primary school there is usually less space for activity. The work is usually divided into separate subjects, perhaps setting children according to ability, and based more on whole-class teaching. Co-operation in group work is encouraged with greater emphasis put on homework and independent learning to develop good work habits. The work is often more wide-ranging, involving new areas, such as a foreign language.

> **Parent quote**
>
> "When my son was given the job of library helper he felt so much better about himself."

Giving privileges and responsibilities makes older children feel special and helps your child get ready to move on to secondary school.

How do children learn about behaviour and getting on with other children?

Learning does not happen only in the classroom. Your child will learn to behave and get on socially with other children at playtimes and at dinner time as well.

Primary schools cover these areas:
- in assembly and religious education
- in 'circle time', a time for younger children to talk and listen to each other about their feelings
- by discussing bad behaviour and playground incidents

Separate lessons in personal and social education, especially for older primary children, may deal with difficult issues like crime or drugs, sometimes working with local police officers or specialist advisers.

Your child will learn most about friendships and right and wrong by growing up in a climate of good relationships and by example from adults and other children.

Parent quote

"I used to find the idea of 'circle time' really strange – but when I helped for a few half days I started to see how the children were able to work together."

Remember!

✔ go to curriculum evenings at school to find out the school's approach to the curriculum

✔ help your child do a wide range of activities

✔ find out about topics your child is studying

✔ support these topics by talking about them, using computers or visiting libraries, museums etc.

How do teachers and parents know how children are getting on?

Your child's class teacher needs to know how well your child is learning in order to work out what to do next. Unless you know, you will not be able to offer help and guidance.

How do they find out?

Assessment is more than just written or oral tests. Tests give only a limited picture. Teachers constantly assess children using:

- ✔ observation
- ✔ discussion
- ✔ written tests

> ### Parent tip
>
> "Set learning targets with your child. If you set them together and agree them your child will probably feel less alone in the whole process."

> ### Parent quote
>
> "We've kept all the school reports from when he started. It's a really good record of his progress – and he likes looking back at them now."

What is the purpose of assessment?

- Teachers often talk about formative assessment. This means working out what problems your child is having, so that schools know how to help and what to concentrate on. This is very useful, and usually time-consuming.

- Most tests and exams are summative assessments. This means that they test what your child has learnt, and can often be used to place children in order. The idea behind them is to encourage children to work hard to pass the test.

- Both formative and summative assessment are important, in different ways. But too much assessment can be discouraging or sometimes even a waste of time.

So how do teachers know what to do next?

When you talk with teachers, try not to concentrate only on problems or just one or two subjects. Try to work out targets, or areas to work on with your child, for the next few months. This is especially important if your child has special educational needs and has an Individual Education Plan (a plan setting out how he or she will be taught).

Can my child be involved?

It can be hard when children are very young, but do try to involve your child in deciding what he or she needs to work hard at. We don't do this enough. Everyone can look back later and see how much progress has been made. Your child may lose confidence or become complacent without some indication of how he or she is progressing.

Talking to teachers

If you don't get much time, or you feel worried between parent-teacher evenings, ask the teacher for an extra discussion. Working out together how to help your child is really important.

Parent quote

"I found it frustrating that we got so little time to talk about our own daughter – I wish the teacher had listened a bit more and said a bit less."

And how do I know how well my child is doing compared to everyone else?

We all want to know this, but do ask yourself, 'How important is this?'. Your own child will know how good everybody in the class is at everything. What really matters is how well your child is doing in relation to his or her potential and compared to previous performance. So target setting is more valuable than putting children in order.

I've heard about 'value added'. What's this all about?

League tables tend to tell us what background children come from, not just how good the school is. To find fair and useful ways to measure how much progress children make at a school – how much the school has 'added on'– is harder. The idea behind Baseline Assessments is to see how well children are doing when they start school, so these later tests can measure how much improvement there has been: **value added**.

What can we learn from the government's tests?

In Year 2 (age seven) and then in Year 6 (age 11), the children are formally assessed by teacher assessment and National Tests in core subjects. These results give scores for your child and school, to compare with local and national figures. Each year, schools' league tables for 11-year-olds are published with targets to raise levels of achievement.

Should I prepare my child for the National Tests?

More schools are spending time getting children to practise for these tests. You will get different views. The tests are not the be-all-and-end-all of success. However, you may want to give your child some practice in the areas to be covered. The school may give advice and there are books providing examples to practise on. There is no easy answer. Remember that the results – good or bad – only measure one part of your child's learning. Try to help your child not to be anxious.

Do children with English as a second language have special assessments?

If your child is learning English as an additional language, he or she is likely to do less well in Year 2 tests in English. By Year 6, most children have caught up. Don't worry too much, unless you think that the school is wrongly assuming your child to be 'slow'. If the scores are low in maths and science and you know he or she has a good understanding, speak to the teachers. Expecting children to do well helps them do well. Assessing your child's ability in the home language is very important, especially for young children.

What about music or art?

Whatever we test tends to become the only thing that matters. These two subjects are very important but we can't easily measure them. It is still important to watch for progress or difficulties and to plan how to build on skills and achievements from year to year.

Remember, watching, talking with and listening to your child is the most important thing you can do to help your child's learning.

My child is worried about moving to secondary school

Children often worry about moving schools. Becoming a small fish in a big pond is quite daunting. Exaggerated stories about bullying or similar may cause real fears. Talk in advance with your child about hopes and worries, including details like the toilets and changing or dinner times and rules. Arrange for a visit on an open day or with the primary school. Often children find the uncertainty hardest to cope with. Seeing the school and the opportunities on offer really helps.

Primary teachers nearly always pass on information about your child's strengths and weaknesses to secondary schools. And usually teachers meet to discuss potential difficulties. If your child has special needs, especially physical disabilities, or is emotionally vulnerable, it may well be worth contacting the secondary school before your child starts. Keep an eye out for how your child settles in the first few vitally important weeks.

Remember!

✔ observe and watch your child's progress over time – don't make snap judgements about his or her progress

✔ talk with other people, especially teachers, about worries and concerns

✔ try not to get too anxious about test results – they tell only part of the story

What special provision can my child expect?

Primary schools offer much more than just what goes on in class. Special provision may be made for:

✔ children with particular abilities or difficulties

✔ children who choose extra activities

What is provided for children with English as an additional language?

The support for your child learning English as an additional language may take place in small groups out of the classroom, or with an extra teacher working alongside the class teacher. Often, this will involve a teacher who speaks your child's first language.

What is provided for children with particular difficulties?

When your child has extra help because of special educational needs, it may be with an adult out of the class, or working in the classroom. This will depend on the sort of help your child needs and how the school chooses to use the support available.

Parent quote

"I wasn't too happy about my child going out of class to learn English – but I think maybe it gave her a little time to get some real individual attention."

Are special arrangements made if my child is very able?

- Some schools have special groups that are doing more demanding work. But usually more able children work in class with more varied or more challenging tasks. If your child performs well across all subjects, make sure, with the teacher, that he or she is getting enough challenging work to maintain interest.

- If your child is able but becomes withdrawn or unhappy, or disruptive, discuss with the teacher how you can modify the work together and set appropriate challenges. High ability children may also have special educational needs, but not necessarily. Each child is different.

Make sure the school responds thoughtfully to the needs of your able child.

Are boys and girls treated differently?

Most schools would answer 'No'. Boys and girls are usually taught together although there is more and more experimentation with separate groups. Most schools try to encourage boys and girls into non-traditional activities – music or fabric work for boys, or technology for girls.

If adults reinforce certain behaviours, children tend to adopt stereotypical roles, so do encourage your child to try out different things. Help boys to play creatively and co-operatively; and girls to be active and assertive.

Boys can have more problems than girls in learning language and in concentrating. They tend to start every stage – talking, reading, writing – later and to have more difficulties. This is partly to do with how the brain works, and partly to do with what society expects of them and the way they behave. You and the teacher may have to work harder for your son to become a successful learner than for your daughter.

Parent quote

"If only we'd shared our worries a little earlier, we might have saved ourselves and our son a lot of heartache catching up with his reading."

What activities are set up for children who choose to take part?

Most primary schools run extra-curricular clubs. These are voluntary and sometimes offered only to older children, partly because they are popular. They are either free or make a small charge for materials. What is provided often depends on teachers' interests, from chess to country-dancing, from sewing to nature study. Probably the most common areas are in music and sport. Remember that teachers lead these voluntarily. Encourage your child to attend regularly.

A word of warning!

Help your child to prioritise out of school activities. Children need time to relax, to reflect and to be with friends – not always doing 'improving' activities!

Do schools offer after-school care?

A growing number of schools offer schemes to look after children after school – to help working parents with childcare and offer a safe, enjoyable environment. Homework clubs and breakfast schemes continue to grow in popularity. If you need this provision, ask if it is available. If not, why not think about helping to set it up?

Parent quote

"On reflection, I think that I pushed Adam into too many after-school activities. He went through a stage of being really irritable and unable to concentrate. I think he was just too tired."

What about trips out of school?

The direct experience offered on day visits and residential trips is an excellent way for your children to learn. You will be asked to pay something towards the cost of many day visits to places of interest, such as museums or farms. These trips are part of the National Curriculum. This is nearly always voluntary, and you don't have to pay. If you are short of money, explain quietly to the teacher that you can't afford it. This won't mean your child can't go, although if lots of parents don't pay schools can't run these trips.

Primary schools often offer older children the chance to go on trips that involve spending a few nights away from home – perhaps outdoor activities or visiting places of interest. Above all, your child will learn to get on with other children and will benefit enormously. The first nights away from home and with friends can be the most memorable time of a child's life. Do send him or her if you can. These longer trips can be quite expensive. But if you are short of money, schools have schemes for reduced prices or free places. So do ask.

Parent quote

"I found that my child really benefitted from the school trips that he went on. It brought him out of himself and gave him confidence. He also made more friends."

Playing an instrument

Many schools still offer the chance to learn a musical instrument. You have to pay for this. But children gain a great deal from learning to read music or playing in a group or orchestra.

Swimming

Swimming is usually provided in the older primary years, although facilities are not available everywhere. The aim is to ensure that your child is a competent, safe swimmer by age 11. This is one enjoyable area where you can probably help out of school with weekend trips to the pool.

Parent quote

"My wife insisted that I teach Liz to swim when she was very little. It really helped her because so many of the school trips – and even out of school visits to friends' houses – involved swimming."

Remember

✔ find out about extra provision if your child speaks English as an additional language

✔ find out about extra provision for children with special needs

✔ help boys to play creatively and co-operatively, and girls to be active and assertive

How are primary schools governed?

Do I really need to know?

You don't need to be an expert but it helps to know a little about how schools are run. You may find that you can make a contribution.

The government makes major decisions about schools, for example on how much money is available and, increasingly, on how your child is taught.

The LEA deals with issues affecting the local area such as special needs, admissions and transport. The LEA only becomes involved in smaller matters if the school cannot solve the problem.

The headteacher and governors are responsible for most aspects of the school and work closely together. The headteacher is responsible for the day-to-day running of the school. He or she makes most of the decisions to keep the school running smoothly and sorts out problems. The headteacher is very important in determining the overall direction and ethos of the school. In most primary schools, you will find that he or she is happy to talk to you.

Find out who to approach

If you have a suggestion or a query, speak first to your child's teacher or to the school office. The school prospectus should suggest how to deal with more serious matters which might affect the whole school, for example persistent bullying or danger from traffic.

If in doubt, contact the headteacher. A good headteacher will always want to sort things out quickly and sensitively.

If you feel worried – especially about your child's progress – speak to your child's teacher. If this doesn't solve the problem, or it is a sensitive issue, you may want to approach a senior member of staff. Often this will be the headteacher, though in larger schools the deputy may be appropriate. And if your child has special educational needs, the special needs co-ordinator may be best.

Remember, if you are unhappy, talk to someone.

Who are the governors? What do they do?

The governors are representatives of the local community. A list is available at the school. There are usually several elected parent governors and there is always an elected teacher along with representatives of local bodies, such as the Church or the LEA.

The governors are volunteers, and usually meet formally once or twice a term. Much of their work is done by committees, deciding on overall policy on the curriculum, buildings, staff and so on. One important area is how the money allocated to the school should be spent.

> **Parent quote**
>
> "I never really found out who the governors were or what they did. We weren't ever told what they actually talked about."

> **Remember**
>
> ✔ find out who to approach if you have a suggestion or a complaint
>
> ✔ if you are unhappy, tell someone. Don't keep it to yourself
>
> ✔ work with the head and governors to improve your school

How do I know what's going on?

The minutes of governors' meetings are usually available. There is an annual report and meeting for parents, when the governors report what they have done on areas such as the budget or perhaps the action plan after a school inspection.

Can I speak direct to the governors?

Yes, of course. But on most matters you should approach the teacher or headteacher first. The governors will usually refer you to the headteacher anyway, but don't be put off asking difficult questions if you are really unhappy about something.

What about school rules?

Most primary schools try to keep formal rules to a minimum and they are usually set out in the prospectus. They may cover things from uniform to what to put in a lunchbox. Help your child by sticking to them. Of course there are all sorts of other informal 'rules', especially among the children!

What are the rules about my child going to school?

You are responsible for ensuring that your child attends school:

✔ regularly (unless you have made separate arrangements)

✔ punctually

I've heard of home-school contracts. What are they?

Schools have to make agreements with parents about responsibilities to ensure that children attend punctually and behave well. Many of these responsibilities are simply based on common sense and courtesy.

Ensure your child doesn't miss school except for illness or a really important reason. And be punctual! It is both rude and disruptive to arrive late, and your child may be blamed for it.

There is no absolute rule on taking holidays during term time, but two weeks in a year should be seen as a maximum. You should get written consent before doing so.

Schools are, rightly, concerned for your child's health and safety. You would expect the school to tell you if your child has been hurt or goes missing. Help the school by telling them when your child is absent. It can save a lot of time and worry.

Parent tips and quotes

"Always stick to school rules and regulations – even if they seem petty – for the sake of your child."

"I forgot to tell the school that Tess was going to be away for one day. Her teachers were very concerned about her and I realised that we'd wasted a lot of their time. Now I always let them know if Tess isn't going to be there."

A typical home-school contract looks like this:

FOR THE SCHOOL.

We, both as individual staff and as a whole school, will:

- provide a safe, well ordered and caring environment

- have clear aims and learning objectives for all pupils

- demonstrate that each and every pupil is valued as an individual

- inform you at an early stage of any concerns we may have so that you can get involved in any matter relating to your child

- ensure we are available to discuss your child's progress or your concerns

- provide opportunities for you to express your views on school issues and have those views listened to

- have a clearly stated behaviour policy detailing expectations, rewards and sanctions

- ensure that school policies are understood and followed by staff, children and parents

FOR THE PARENT.

As a parent of a pupil at the school I/we will:

- support my child's learning, including ensuring the completion of any homework set

- encourage my child to read, and hear her/him read on a regular basis

- support the school in maintaining high standards of behaviour by supporting the school's behaviour policy

- respond to any reasonable request by the school to discuss my child's education

- ensure regular attendance and a high standard of punctuality

- ensure my child has what he or she needs to take a full part in all activities

- comply with the school's Uniform Code

FOR THE PUPIL.

As a pupil I will:

- show that I am willing to work to the best of my ability

- always behave in a way that enables all children to work and play without interference or harm

- try to get on with others in the school community

- have and keep tidily the books and equipment I need for my lessons, including P.E. and games kit

- encourage my parent(s) to be involved with my learning

- take pride in my appearance and wear school uniform

- come to school regularly and on time

- help ensure that the school is a pleasant environment in which to work and play by keeping it clean, tidy and free from litter

How can I get involved?

An enjoyable aspect of having a child at primary school can be getting involved in school activities. How much you do this depends on your own interests and other commitments. Don't feel guilty if other parents are more involved than you. But make sure you are involved in supporting your own child's progress wherever you can.

Most schools encourage parents (or other relatives) to help in school. This might be by:

✔ helping individuals or groups of children

✔ running a chess club or a sports session

✔ one-off events such as giving a talk about your job or somewhere you've visited

✔ accompanying children on school visits or helping with transport

✔ offering a particular skill like fixing computers

If you are keen, do volunteer. Schools are usually very grateful and you will probably enjoy helping out.

Parent quote

"The socials at my daughter's school were brilliant – barbecues, dances, treasure hunts, things like that. It was how we made most of our friends – and that was ten years ago."

PTAs

There is often a parent-teacher association (PTA) or 'Friends of...' committee.
They may arrange:

✔ educational events with visiting speakers

✔ social events like barndances or quizzes

✔ fundraising events like fairs or auctions

These days, the main focus is on raising money for the school. But these groups are a good chance to make friends.

Parent quote

"I'd not thought of standing as parent governor. But when I saw the vacancy, I thought I'd try. I never imagined how many decisions there were for the governors to take."

Often schools invite parents in for assemblies to see children's work and for big religious festivals, such as Harvest or Easter, Diwali or Eid. The most effort is usually put into a service or play at Christmas. These are often very enjoyable and memorable occasions.

You will probably be invited to events like sports days or end-of-year plays or concerts. These are usually good fun with both children and teachers putting in a lot of hard work.

Most primary schools have occasional evening meetings. These may be to talk about an aspect of the curriculum, the annual meeting for parents, or the meeting before an OFSTED inspection.

You may want to become a governor. The amount of commitment varies, but can be considerable. Most schools are on the lookout for keen parents to be governors. Talk to the headteacher or chair of governors if you are interested.

What if I don't have time for all these things?

Choose how much you want to be involved in all of these. If you can't join a group it will help if you:

- ✔ read to and with your child

- ✔ show an interest in what has happened at school

- ✔ check on and help with homework when needed

- ✔ help your child to be independent and organised

If your child says that the work is too hard ('I don't understand') or too easy ('I'm bored'), keep your eyes open. Don't rush in straight away, but consider whether to go and see the teacher.

Parent quote

"Looking back, I don't think he'd have made the transition to secondary school so easily if we hadn't really insisted on him settling to homework in the last year of primary."

How should I support my child through primary school?

It is difficult to strike the balance between maintaining an interest and the right amount of pressure, and not fussing or nagging too much. As your child gets older, he or she will become more independent and resilient. Encourage this, but remain interested and available.

THREE DIFFICULT AREAS CAN BE:

✔ Friendships. You can't determine who your child's friends will be. But you can encourage friendships, especially if your child is a bit of a loner. Gently discourage unsuitable friends, especially if your child is getting into trouble. Be careful though – this can be counter-productive!

✔ Homework. Most schools want parents to help children do some extra work at home. With young children this is often with reading. Later on, it may involve spelling or maths, and at the top end of primary school more independent, project-based work. When children are young, establishing routines and expectations is easier. This is harder when your child is nine or ten, unless you have already built up this pattern.

Getting involved

✔ offer your time or skills to your child's school if you can

✔ think about being a governor or active on the PTA

✔ don't feel guilty if you are less involved than other parents

✔ establish routines and expectations when your child is quite young

✔ encourage your child to be independent and resilient, but remain interested and available

✔ get involved when there's a problem with behaviour or bullying

✔ Behaviour and discipline. You must get involved when there's a problem. Don't believe all your child says, but do take notice and look out for patterns suggesting bullying or misbehaviour. Listen and watch out for clues such as your child becoming withdrawn, bored or stroppy. If it goes on for any length of time, try to find out what's going on.

Be prepared to act promptly if your child is being bullied or is getting into trouble. If the school contacts you about punishment, take it seriously. Parental support is essential, usually to back up the school, or to find out what has happened. If bad behaviour isn't sorted out quickly, it can lead to serious problems.

Most children find primary school very exciting. Your child will make friends, do interesting things and make fantastic progress in the primary years. Try to share in this and enjoy being part of the wider school community. Many parents and children rightly look back on the years in primary school with great affection.

Enjoy your child growing into a confident, enthusiastic and independent learner.

Glossary

Agreed Syllabus   A document drawn up locally by various different faith communities and the LEA to decide what Religious Education should be taught.

Attainment Targets   Targets for children's learning in each subject at different stages. Each Attainment Target is divided into eight levels, like steps up a ladder.

Baseline Assessment   Teacher observation of children within the first seven weeks of entering the Reception class, which is used to assess learning levels in maths, English and social skills.

Catchment area   Officially the area around a school where parents have priority in admissions. Often used loosely to mean the area where the children live.

Church schools   Schools founded with a religious basis, but within the state system. There are various types, the main differences being in religious education and admissions for church aided schools. Most were founded by the Church of England or the Roman Catholic Church.

Core subjects   The main subjects in the National Curriculum: English, maths and science. R.E. (religious education) and I.C.T. (Information and Communications Technology) are also treated like core subjects. These are the only subjects where set Programmes of Study have to be taught in full.

Daily Maths Lesson   The time each day which schools devote to teaching mathematics, especially numeracy (working with numbers).

Information and Communications Technology (I.C.T.)   The term to replace I.T. (Information Technology) meaning the use of computers and other electronic means to enhance learning.

Key Stages   Stages at which a child's education can be assessed, after following a Programme of Study. There are four Key Stages, dividing ages 5-7, 7-11, 11-14 and 14-16.

Literacy Hour – the time each day which schools have to devote to teaching literacy skills.

Local Education Authority (LEA)   The county, borough or district education authority. LEAs have many specific roles especially in admissions, finance and special educational needs.

National Curriculum   The government's system of education, broken into four Key Stages, which applies to all pupils of compulsory school age in maintained schools. It contains core and foundation (non-core) subjects, and incorporates National Tests at the end of each Key Stage.

National Tests   Tests taken in school at the end of each Key Stage – at ages 7, 11 and 14 – to determine what Attainment Target pupils have reached. The scores are also used – especially at age 11 – to compare the results of schools as a whole.

OFSTED (Office for Standards in Education)   The government department which oversees inspections and sends teams to assess individual schools.

Parent-teacher association (PTA) The group of parents, teachers and others who support the school in various social, educational and fundraising ways. It may be called by a different name and may or may not be associated with the national group of PTAs.

Prospectus/brochure The booklet produced by a school to describe how it works and what it provides.

'Rising fives' Children in the term before that in which their fifth birthday falls.

Setting Placing children of similar ability level together for a particular subject.

Streaming Placing children of similar ability level together for all subjects.

Teacher Assessment The teacher's own judgements about the level of progress children have made. This is a part of deciding both what and how to teach, and also takes place more formally at set times, especially with the National Tests at 7 and 11 years old.

Value added An attempt to measure how much progress a child has made in a set period between two assessments.

USEFUL INFORMATION

Advisory Centre for Education (ACE)
Department A, Unit 1B Aberdeen Studios,
22 Highbury Grove, London N5 2DQ
Web: www.ace-ed.org.uk/
Phone: 020 7354 8321
Free advice, information and support for parents of children in state schools.

Basic Skills Agency
7th Floor, Commonwealth House,
1-19 New Oxford Street, London WC1A 1NU
Web: www.basic-skills.co.uk/
Phone: 020 7405 4017
National development agency for basic literacy and numeracy skills.

British Association for Early Childhood Education (BAECE)
136 Cavell Street, London E1 2SA
Web: www.early-education.org.uk
Phone: 020 7539 5400

DfEE (Department for Education and Employment)
Sanctuary Buildings, Great Smith Street,
London SW1P 3BT
Web: www.dfee.gov.uk
Phone: 020 7925 5555
Free publications on all aspects of education can be sent, available by phoning 01787 880946.

Education Otherwise
PO Box 7420, London, N9 9SG
Web: www.e-o.users.netlink.co.uk/
Phone: 0891 518 303
For information about pre-school education at home.

National Association for Special Educational Needs
NASEN House, 4/5 Amber Business Village,
Amber Close, Amington, Tamworth B77 4RP
Web: www.nasen.org.uk
Phone: 01827 311 500

National Confederation for Parent Teacher Associations (NCPTA)
2 Ebbsfleet Estate, Stonebridge Road, Gravesend, Kent DA11 9DZ
Web: www.rmplc.co.uk/orgs/ncpta
Phone: 01474 560 618
Promotes partnership between home and school, children, parents, teachers and education authorities.

National Early Years Network
77 Holloway Road, London, N7 8JZ
Phone: 020 7607 9573

Pre-school Learning Alliance (PLA)
69 King's Cross Road, London WC1X 9LL
Web: www.childcare-now.co.uk/psla.html
Phone: 020 7883 0991

WEBSITES

www.basic-skills.co.uk/
The website of Basic Skills, who work with schools to develop basic skills.

www.ace-ed.org.uk/
The website of the Advisory Centre for Education.

www.hometown.aol.com/wiseowlsw
A UK children's specialist in education software to play online or download.

www.bbc.co.uk/education/schools/primary.shtml
Home and school learning resources for children. The BBC education site as a whole has resources to cover a large range of educational issues.